FALSE SPRING

False Spring

Poems
by
GLORIA MONAGHAN

Adelaide Books
New York / Lisbon
2019

FALSE SPRING

Poems

By Gloria Monaghan

Copyright © by Gloria Monaghan

Cover image & design - Frank Navin

Published by Adelaide Books, New York / Lisbon
adelaidebooks.org

Editor-in-Chief
Stevan V. Nikolic

All rights reserved. No part of this book may be reproduced in any manner whatsoever without written permission from the author except in the case of brief quotations embodied in critical articles and reviews.

For any information, please address Adelaide Books
at info@adelaidebooks.org
or write to:
Adelaide Books
244 Fifth Ave. Suite D27
New York, NY, 10001

ISBN-10: 1-950437-07-8
ISBN-13: 978-1-950437-07-8

Printed in the United States of America

To
Johanna Navin Monaghan

In memory of Michael Francis
Cergizon and Herbert S. Scott

Dark house, by which once more I stand
Here in the long unlovely street,
Doors, where my heart was used to beat
So quickly, waiting for a hand

–Alfred, Lord Tennyson,
In Memoriam A.H.H. OBIIT MDCCCXXXIII

Contents

Joy *13*

THE GLISTENING HUDSON RIVER *15*

Cemetery *16*

The Days Pass Like Blue Wheels *17*

Remembering my father and
the sun of New Jersey *18*

Slipper Moon *19*

"Dreams that are Unremembered and
Unspeakable in the Daylight" *21*

Red Flower *22*

Daughter *23*

VICTORY GARDEN *25*

The Park *26*

Birdseed *27*

"There Stands by Grief the Shadow of Love" *28*

Victory Garden *29*

March *30*

Dogfight *31*

Statue of Mary in the Garden *32*

"Don't Accept the Heart that is Slave to Reason" *33*

Resurrection *34*

Venus *35*

VALENTINE POEMS *37*

Valentine Poem #1 *38*

Valentine Poem #2–When 2 Hearts Meet *39*

Valentine Poem #3 *40*

Valentine Poem #4 *41*

Valentine Poem #5–Melody *42*

Valentine Poem #6 *43*

Valentine Poem # 7 *44*

Valentine Poem #8 *45*

YELLOW BACKYARD *47*

Rockport *48*

Christmas Tree *49*

FALSE SPRING

Dance **50**

Ambassador Bridge **52**

Greenfield **53**

Radiation **54**

Christmas **57**

Shadow **58**

King Hercules **59**

Blue Flight **60**

Diveline **61**

Kiss **64**

Pavement **65**

The Hand **67**

Acknowledgments 69

Notes 71

About the Author 75

Joy

Sing, majestic day-camp counselor
    the colors of the flowers
    have given in to green.

THE GLISTENING HUDSON RIVER

Cemetery

I need to be doing some very basic task
like mowing the graveyard grass.
The air is filling with green and the smell of youth
yellow defused weeds
spirit up from the dark death ground.

The Days Pass Like Blue Wheels

Each day in blue darkness
a lonely girl
with small but strong limbs
rises out of bed
thinking that the trees,
which are green, have
powers in themselves to perhaps lift secrets
from their cluttered and knowing branches,
oh caress, caress and tell
what parts of the sky you have touched.

Remembering my father and the sun of New Jersey

The memory comes in patches and disappears.
A John Coltrane song playing
in the hills of black neighborhoods
laundry on the line
cement blocks resting on the grass.

He was driving from the back seat I see
the empty beige color of his raincoat,
folded pack of Newports
the green light of the car radio saxophone and
exhaust of Greyhound buses in New York City,
and the dull gray glisten of the Hudson River.

Slipper Moon

Older sister smokes her cigarette
black coffee half filled
crossword on her lap
faint orange lipstick from the night before
across her slightly sensuous lips.

Brother in his Italian tee
brown spots over the once muscular shoulders
black curly hair
dark brow, paper folded,
with dime-store glasses in his hand.

Little sister wears socks on the couch
one pinky finger extended forever
from a kitchen accident
brush in her lap
silver and black streaked hair.

Smoke rises to the ceiling,
brother starts to swear about politics
and is forced upstairs

like a child who has committed a small crime.
Upstairs, the TV picks up where it left off .

The siblings have drifted far from their previous lives. How
intricate the night, branch against the window,
bird careful in the gutter, looking twice into the small nest.
The dog asleep on his ravaged bed
between the bathroom and the basement stairs.

Little sister's hands twine long, delicate strands of hair,
her eyes rest on the slipper moon outside.

"Dreams that are Unremembered and Unspeakable in the Daylight"

Fortune Cookie

He kissed me in front of the Puerto Rican bakery
with all the people around us
in the blaring twelve o'clock sun
and hair in our mouths.

I walked away from the highway.
Today, beneath the buildings
everyone is in love and the sky is shattering
clouds are moving across the parking lot,
and if there is love, it is orange.

Red Flower

Love is a hard rock.
My heart is in you
your mouth is telling me all about blue
I am waiting in a little house with a sparse green garden
and a red flower in the middle.
Small lizards run out in the sun
and under the porch where they live.
In the dead of night sometime we all woke,
you, the baby, and I
and looked out into the moonlight,
our dark bed surrounded by night.
A white cat beneath the window
just waiting and looking and waiting in the darkness.
We wondered about the meaning of the white spirit cat.
I am waiting in the cottage house.

Daughter

The smell of my daughter's hair breaks my heart.
It is the smell of the creek, dirt, green ferns, and
breath of the depleting hours of summer
new trees
and the coast.
It is the smell of departure.

VICTORY GARDEN

The Park

The park in the middle of the city sits.

How many cats have trailed through undespised?

Birdseed

She lifted the stick
and they all flew
into the street;
then she turned,
her small poodle clothed
in layers of coats, and sneered at me
at the gray streetlight.

I walked beneath the pigeons.
We are all part of a bird's game.
She threw the bread.
I crossed the street
beyond the water, beyond the reeds,
my heart torn to pieces.

"There Stands by Grief the Shadow of Love"

Fortune Cookie

Empty bed, artful heart
I will call her a blue vein
I will summon her from the waters
like an unfathomable blue hope silent under skin.

Someone robbed her of her only son
someone silent, beneath, behind, between
flowers smiling
knees deep in the water of despair;
cradled hands.

On a summer day
the girl turns in the aqua water
hot pink bathing suit
tattoos flashing
laughing
her hair like snakes
off her head.
She claps her hands
spins her legs
to stay afloat in the transparent blue.

Victory Garden

The lilac dust of cut flowers
falls malignant upon our shoulders
and we swear it will never happen again.
All that we begrudge
fits into a cat's paw.

March

> *"Life is a series of suicides, divorces, promises
> broken, children smashed, whatever."*
> —Love Streams, John Cassavetes

The police search the reeds and the water
in the Victory Garden
in the hope of finding a body.

The water freezes and unfreezes continually.
The ducks stay beneath the bridge.
One boy in a ski jacket
throws snow at them that are so hungry.

Did your body smell like an ocean?
Did we ever go to the drive-in together?
Your body is a place to get lost in
the sun burns away all our fear.

Dogfight

The sky has a memory the birds sing it;
yellow November leaves fall
piteously to the ground. Walking in the park
a pack of boys, a dogfight, glass in flesh, a reason
for the park to turn carelessly brown on a yellow cold day.
The air a vortex, the leaves vanish.
Noonday branches
go up forever and ever
propelling tiny black answers
they reassure all who ask of it,
they give those empty spaces
light and blue
praise the never-failing sky.

Statue of Mary in the Garden

My idiot veil separates the world from the interior one.
Crushed flowers deteriorate in the dry room.
Sudden renewal in the garden of
deception, the Victory Garden
blue-veined eyelids can pretend nothing
merciless hand dancing in the wind.

Where does pity end?
Butterflies, transfiguration
imagined caress, imagined forgiveness
the hand of gratitude covets the other.
A grotesque gesture withering in the empty vase.

Flawed smiles finished in youth
abandoned and forgotten
still the moonlight spreads.
The immobile heart a sad storm,
the wind your tears.

"Don't Accept the Heart that is Slave to Reason"

Fortune Cookie

I have spent the year defining the park in terms of my heart
and nothing has come of it but the reeds,
which come up loose and green every spring.
That September I reigned in your mind
that February the wind shook the trees brightly
we embraced on the curbs
hitting the fenders of automobiles; we embraced
in doorways, lifted our tongues in our hollow mouths,
we abandoned the season.

Resurrection

Frail shadows of yellow weeds
swaying in the seven o'clock wind.

Venus

For the moment we are trying our best to
trapeze desire
and say life goes
on and on and on and on
find the rose find the agony find the deliberation.
Venus is burning, does anyone know how
to burn so brightly? Firebird, queer
half the park comes to burn at 12:20 on a Friday
silently smoking delicately dying.
The strong black trees of paradise
stand up gawking.
In the daylight the grass and leaves
divide and sing divide and sing divide and sing.

VALENTINE POEMS

Valentine Poem #1

Your smell escapes me.
You don't want to give up your shirt
and I don't want to take it.
Lovers are always claiming each other with clothes.
As if the smell would ever stay the same way
as if our smiles would not be revealed in the Puerto Rican
bakery, under the fluorescent light.

Valentine Poem #2–When 2 Hearts Meet

I was engaged to Gus Farance.
He was trying to kill me.
My mother was living in his house.
I ran with the rope
through the wet green forests that
surround the Rouge River,
the extension of our souls.
Why is everything polluted in
the rock mud of the river bed?

Valentine Poem #3

The park is covered with bright and terrible hard snow.
The alarm clock perpetually stoned
blinking red and red.
The angels have nowhere to go
and when we do see them, fallen, with their old
heads bleeding, we look the other way.

The man in the Arabic store of refuge tells you
to call from a payphone.
Stupefied, we sit with our hands in our laps.
Our father on the corner, drunk
waiting, tongue-tied.

In the food store of romance
two or three mice scatter here and there
our world inside Marlborough Market enlarges to infinity
in the curved mirrors
our curved smiles
delirious and consumed we march from one
harlequin dream sheet to the Pizza Pad.
Julie Christie, where are you?

Valentine Poem #4

Across the viaduct someone has spray-painted
Are you trying to blame me?
There is a Japanese reply,
when the snow falls it becomes more significant.

In the bird store there are a few canaries;
although the origin of the birds is neglected
their eminent history remains—birdbrain.

How can anyone ask another to trust him or her as the world
falls so prettily upon their shoulders
from the vast, glittering uranium skies?

We forget our bona fide reward,
the embrace,
the love of another.

Valentine Poem #5–Melody

Blue divine dream
where are you,
enclosed in a sheer body bag, embalmed
in someone else's heart—
Who is that knocking downstairs?
The daylight
never ceases to astonish
sometimes silver, or light orange,
as if that's all we need.

Valentine Poem #6

Did I enjoy keeping bad thoughts in my mind?
How many times?
How many times?

Saint Christopher is with us.
We are not listed as
contagious to one another and still
we read the same books.

Frank O'Hara gallantly walking down a Puerto Rican street
wondering what to bring to a dinner party
(at the same time the sky was on fire).
The corner of an upturned smile,
there was a flicker of happiness
at the line of the eye.

Valentine Poem #7

Apollo's lover bloodied the ground forever.
We ruin what we love we love what we ruin.
The sun shines a certain way in New Orleans
that doesn't exist anywhere else.
The dreams that evade me have centered on my shoulders
and that is what my body aches.

Valentine Poem #8

Between the walls—unhinged
it's easy to walk through Southern streets
on a rainy day in New Orleans past the bent splintering
doorways and pillars of romance,
railings of sinister despair
into the Warehouse District, where
everything comes together on the corner with the groceries,
a cigarette and a smile at the truck driver.

YELLOW BACKYARD

Rockport

On the train from the city to the coast
you kiss my neck with your warm cat-like tongue
the salt from the skin in
your mouth like the taste of blood.

Lilac dust
intrinsic wordplay beloved
violet damaged boy of twenty-five.

Christmas Tree

I dreamt about your kisses
the menagerie of petals
falling white into white
snow and sky are filled
with horns, and Chet Baker
is dying with a plea
and a force
of fire like a long
dwindling light falling
off the Christmas tree
dust of a thousand souls
collapsing on top of each other
a trumpet and a dangle of laughter.
Keep going, keep dangling, trip me up.

Dance

Snow covers the ground
the black outlines of trees
divide the early morning.

We feed the birds and wait
they won't come so close
to the window where the small tin
is placed on the ledge.

Sunlight fades in the sky
late morning
people discuss
food and their jobs
voices barely interfering with the snow.

The winter like a gloved hand over my face.
You sell our songs from New Orleans.
The one about the black cat,
the one about the iron rails.

We drift by cafés
drink coffee, dance in discos,

FALSE SPRING

whiskey breath, hand on the wheel
dancing together, face to face,
drawing from each other.

Ambassador Bridge

After dinner at the Clark Room, with
Bessie Smith on the radio
over the Ambassador Bridge, it occurs
to me that nothing is safe.
The steel spirals just suspended over hundreds of feet of water
are like my hand over the face of a cat,
a web of restriction useless to the animal.
The music is playing, my mother and aunt are talking;
no one suspects anything.

Greenfield

Like children we return to what we know
tripping on the same crack in the sidewalk
you're leaning against a wall
you tell me this is the gateway to downriver
and you are being carried down
the river of forgetfulness, the River Styx,
the Rouge River of Detroit
past factories, Belle Isle where you
used to go with your brother
to the Grand Prix to eat Coney Islands.
Your hands white and callused
the weary expression of green in your eyes
eyebrows raised in mock surprise, mouth unrevealing.

We talked on the bridge over Grand River
the cars below fast and the police passing us
once they saw in our eyes the sorrow of the young.
You were saying something
but I wasn't listening. I was looking at
the cars beneath the flash of headlights
the regret of taillights
beneath the bridge.

Radiation

You let me brush your hair.
I brush and carefully fold it together
so compliant you sit, like my child,
your back straight, silent.
You look beautiful when I finish.

Recently on the telephone,
recalling some unspeakable crime,
you are barely able to answer.

In a dream you played the piano in an old people's home
on Grandville in the lobby.
You were singing a song by Teenage Fanclub.
I heard it from the balcony and sang it with you.
I sat on the stairs and looked at you in
your green ragged clothing.

You were gone already even though you were there.
You asked me if I had been to The Granada lately
which proves you're insane
because the Granada was torn down ten years ago
and is now a parking garage.

FALSE SPRING

I remember The Granada,
the small white statues along the width
and glory of the facade,
and I remember seeing Johnny Rotten there with you.
We walked down the aisle and he was singing
in a fabulous orange plaid suit.

But I knew it was my imagination
because we listened from the alley.
We had no money for tickets and
you weren't even there.

It has recently occurred to me you must
have been my daughter once,
though you are still here in Albuquerque,
where the dead grass borders adobe homes,
coffee shops, radiation, big cars, and
graves of Indians.

In the last line of the dream
you are coming to me with a smile on your face
saying *my angel, my angel …*
And I was waiting for you like a husband.
It was getting late and you had been drinking all day.

The cycles of hell never really end,
another cycle of despair
gone it's four o'clock.

Gloria Monaghan

You're not coming back.
Of all the feelings, do you know that one
abandonment
at four o'clock
in an old people's home?

I forgot what you said
moving away from all of us
in the radiation.

Christmas

Ingrid Bergman against the El Greco sky
survives Bing Crosby in front of the black
cemetery fence

deluge, demise; love.
The nuns huddle as she leaves. Pigeon-like nuns
cruel gazes and hurtful words, they guide her
sadness.

The washboards of New Orleans moan.

Shadow

Something about our breath—
is there a sweeter taste?

Throw coins in the air
your back has a shadow
emblazoned across it
I am walking through
somehow.

King Hercules

Not quite bitter, broken, or green,
more like glittered aqua and driven,
she saunters down her own steps
neither confident nor free.
In the street they drag the limp junkie
from the apartment complex,
the police wearing white plastic gloves.
She looks to the evening sky,
then looks away because
in the constellations,
the heart is a giant hook
capturing, pulling a bloody corpse with it.

Blue Flight

Adrenaline
lifeboat
blue robe
dove eyes
embrace of a thousand lives
and within
the folds
blue night upon blue stars
scattered diamonds.

Goodbye daydream
unaffected memory, destroyer.

Diveline

I

The lake is murky.
He is at the bottom, but I will find him in darkness,
the other lifeguards and I; all of us in a perfect line
like a dove's tail waist deep in the water.
He acquiesced to sink, four-year-old lungs filling fast
betraying the body weight, no more than a lakeshore stone
endlessly falling through the moss green
wavering above the sand line.

II

The pool is empty
water smooth like a baby's belly
full of expectation.
Under what circumstance does betrayal occur?
Separating water with my palms
a calm prophet
turning aqua air
still water with false hope
the depth so alluring
one false move
a moment of panic

loss of control.
Yet the torso does not fail
continues to glide; arms, legs, mind, eyes
an automated machine
one moment is all it takes
for everything to go wrong in a lifetime.

III

Under the x-ray machine
the baby screamed.
Her head looked like it would crush.
For a moment I believed her
tiny outrageous scream
her new teeth shining
small curved pearls
cheeks red and puffy like some great cherry about to split.
We understood the machine would not fall on her
but we did not believe.
The nurses pricked her hands with needles
to inject the serum.
Instead of looking away we
stared as if we could change it
all the while thinking
what do they know
that we need to know
why are they talking about condos?
Who is the man in the wheelchair

FALSE SPRING

in Nuclear Medicine,
with his face already dead,
in striped pajamas.

In the machine hum we are powerless.

Kiss

Open your heart to the color of desire
give me your hand
walk the only courtyard after the
sun and people go

notice the white stone glimmers so silently
and you thought
it was cold
it is only the moon
piercing your skin

it is only my fingers
touching your back
making the soft
boy-hairs on the back of your neck
stand up.

It is only a whisper that passes
as a shadow that lingers
like a torn muscle through you.

Pavement

You wonder about ghosts and their whereabouts,
especially out of season.
On a mid-March day in January
under the quick glance of a stranger
you romanticize that you are being followed
by one of your dead lovers.
He is next to you on the bus, and
you've resumed the old
unfinished, rehashed conversation.
He grows tired quickly and excuses himself.

Gray tombstones stand out against the gray air.
Trees dark, ancient outlines.
The humid stillness of air makes you
think of New Orleans.
The turgid, dire, wet, completely
hopeless streets are exactly the same.

Yesterday, I thought I saw you with a
haircut you had five years ago
five years younger, with an old girlfriend

Gloria Monaghan

smiling that strange smile—
laughing at something else,
yet smiling at the beauty of the dark pavement.

The Hand

The hand I dreamt of was light brown
it held nothing
it was relaxed and warm
it soothed me to look at it
a small stone
a swan's neck
a leaf
tomorrow.

Acknowledgments

"Statue in the Garden": University of Illinois at Chicago, Electronic Visualization Laboratory, 2003.

"The Days Pass Like Blue Wheels": *Chaffin Journal,* 2002.

Cover Art by Frank Navin.

Thanks to Ron Bernier for his support and Wentworth Institute of Technology for providing me with a sabbatical to work on this project. Special thanks to editor, Cindy Hochman of "100 Proof" Copyediting Services.

Notes

Herbert S. Scott was a poet at WMU and founder editor of *New Issues Press.*

Michael F. Cergizon was a musician and poet based in Chicago and Kalamazoo.

"That September I reigned in your mind," "Sleeping Analeah," Nick Cave

"Valentine Poem #2: 'Gus' Farance (1960–1989) worked for the Colombo crime family. He murdered a teenage male prostitute and a federal agent in New York City.

"Valentine Poem #6: "How many times" is a reference to Rev. Alphonse Sausen's book *Pray Always, Prayers and Instruction for Children,* Catholic Book Publishing Co., 1961. Print.

"Ambassador Bridge": Suspension bridge that connects Windsor, Ontario, to Detroit.

"Greenfield": This poem takes place on Joy Road in Detroit, outside the punk rock/gay bar called Nunzio's (now defunct).

The Granada Theater on Sheridan Road in Chicago was built in the 1920s by the Marx Brothers. It was a beautiful historic building that was demolished in the early 1990s.

The poem "Christmas," references *The Bells of St. Mary's*, a 1945 film starring Ingrid Bergman and Bing Crosby

"King Hercules": A reference to LL Cool J.

"Diveline": A term I heard lifeguards using to find the body of a small boy on Lake Michigan.

"Pavement": This poem also alludes to the band Pavement and music I was listening to at the time.

About the Author

Gloria Monaghan is a Professor of Humanities at Wentworth Institute in Boston. She has published two books of poetry, *Flawed* (Finishing Line Press, 2011, nominated for the Massachusetts Book Award) and *The Garden* (Flutter Press 2015). Her poem "Into Grace" won the 2018 Adelaide Voices Poetry Award. Her poems have appeared in *Adelaide, the Aurorean, Aries, Blue Max Review, Fox Chase, 2River,* and *Underground Writer's Association,* among others.

www.ingramcontent.com/pod-product-compliance
Lightning Source LLC
Chambersburg PA
CBHW020254090426
42735CB00010B/1920